Little Rhody
&
The Other 49

*A look at some of the more
fascinating points about
49 of our states and how
Rhode Island compares*

by
Roberta Mudge Humble

Thanks to PrintShops, Inc. of Cliff Street, East Greenwich, Rhode Island for the fine quality of this printing.

ISBN 978-0-9838292-0-1

Printed in the
State of Rhode Island and Providence Plantations
UNITED STATES OF AMERICA
10 9 8 7 6 5 4 3 2 1

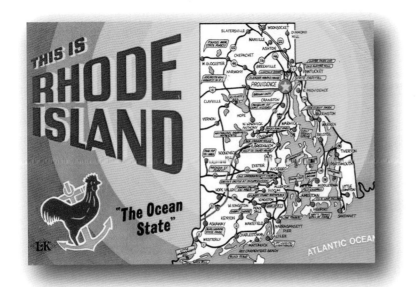

Welcome to Rhode Island, the smallest state with the longest name. Your author is a native Rhode Islander, author of books and trivia games about Rhode Island – and a proud citizen of the state, ready to show you why Rhode Islanders like living here.

Rhode Island's Roger Williams established the first practical working model of democracy and a home for religious freedom. Who would not be proud of that?

On the lighter side, in Rhode Island, low-numbered license plates are a status symbol. The record in the nation paid for one of these was $25,000 – right in Rhode Island.

Rhode Islanders don't eat clams; they eat quahogs – and the quahog is the state animal (and the longest-lived aquatic animal – up to 405 years).

The state name is the longest in the nation – *Rhode Island and Providence Plantations* – and our state motto is the shortest – *Hope*. Citizens take pride being first or last at anything. Rhode Island is now the only state to celebrate VJ Day, now called "Victory Day," marking the end of World War II.

Rhode Islanders consider having to stay overnight in a hotel if they drive to the other side of the state. Many Rhode Island citizens own beach houses less than an hour away from their permanent homes.

Left: Cogswell Tower (Central Falls) & Slater Mill (Pawtucket) over-nighting in Middletown. From Rhode Island's Friendly Faces.

When a snowflake falls, Rhode Islanders load up on bread and milk. They use landmarks, even long-demolished landmarks, when giving driving directions.

In spite of what everyone thinks, the Industrial Trust Tower (now Bank of America) on the Providence skyline was <u>not</u> the model for the Daily Planet building in the Superman series. However, many people call it the "Superman building."

Being six degrees removed from anyone else is a common notion; however, Rhode Islanders are only *two* degrees removed. It is a state where you are known by your Governor, US Senator, and US Congressman. Rhode Island has 5 counties, 39 cities & towns, 12 colleges, 14 state parks, 18 historic armories, over1200 registered farms, and 400 miles of coastline. Sixty percent of Rhode Island is forested.

Rhode Island was the site of the first national lawn tennis championship and is home to the Tennis Hall of Fame – and it was also the site of the first roller skating rink in America.

Rhode Islanders pronounce "idea" with an "r" at the end, but drop the "r" on "car." They don't say "down town," they say "down city." They don't have drinking fountains, they have bubblers. Sometimes, they even pronounce the acronym for the Rhode Island Public Transportation Authority as "Ripter."

RHODE ISLAND PUBLIC TRANSIT AUTHORITY

Take a look at Rhode Island while you also get a peek at Rhode Island's 49 brother states, as impressive in their own way. Be ready for a large dose of American pride.

ALABAMA is home to the Air War College and the famous statue of the Boll Weevil. Huntsville, Alabama workers built the first rocket, the Saturn V, to put a man on the moon. Alabama is the rocket capital of the nation and known for its programs on the space shuttle and international space station.

6

On its behalf, **Rhode Island** built the first water-powered cotton mill in the nation which began the Industrial Revolution in America. This was created by Samuel Slater; the mill was named for him, Slater Mill.

ALASKA's capital, Juneau is the only state capital which is accessible *only* by boat or plane. Alaska has one of the *lowest* population densities of the 50 states.

Rhode Island has one of the *highest* population densities. Alaska, the 49th state, is so large that 425 Rhode Islands could fit inside it.

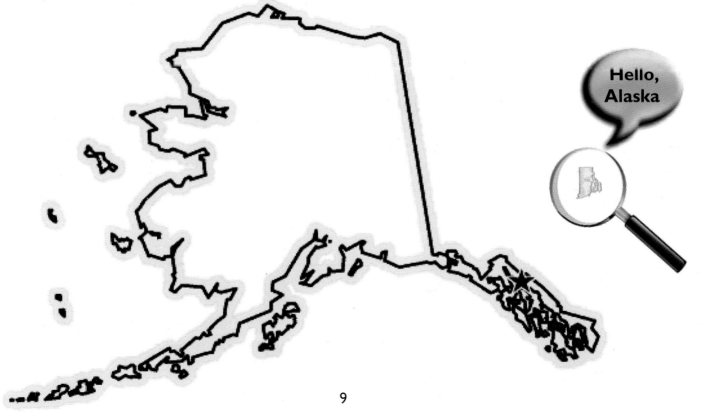

9

ARIZONA, home of the Grand Canyon, is also home to London Bridge in Lake Havsu City, bought and brought in pieces from London, England.

Rhode Island boasts a statue of the Independent Man which was created from a statue of Simon Bolivar, taken from New York's Central Park – broken up, melted down, and cast by Rhode Island's Gorham Manufacturing Company, pre-eminent silversmiths in America. The Independent Man sits atop Rhode Island's State House.

11

ARKANSAS, home of the famous mineral baths at Hot Springs and home of the World Championship Duck Calling Contest (Stuttgart), can boast the first WalMart store in the nation in 1962. Bentonville is now the site of corporate headquarters.

Sam Walton's 5 & 10 store, now the WalMart Visitors' Center

Historic Bath Houses at Hot Springs

Before that, in 1953 in **Rhode Island**, Martin and Irwin Chase created Ann & Hope, the first major self-service discount store in the nation which included the first time central check-out as well as shopping carts were used in a department store — and offering the first night-time hours (9 am to 10pm) as well as free parking. Most inventive.

13

Ann&Hope

CALIFORNIA, home of Hollywood stars and the floral elegance of the Rose Bowl Parade, is the site of the largest living tree, a Sequoia, at Sequoia National Park with a trunk of 103 feet in circumference.

14

On the east side of the Mississippi River, it is Bristol, **Rhode Island** that has the tallest Sequoia tree with a slightly smaller circumference. In addition, Rhode Island has the oldest Fourth of July celebration in the nation with patriotic exercises, a parade of patriotism, and a stripe on the parade route of red, white, and blue.

Sequoia tree at Blithewold in Bristol
Inspected by the Old Windmill

Left: Pawtuxet Rangers march in the Fourth of July Parade

COLORADO, home to the Air Force Academy and with more microbreweries per capita than any other state, is the site of Pike's Peak which was the inspiration for Katherine Lee Bates to write "America the Beautiful."

16

5. America, the Beautiful

Katharine Lee Bates   Samuel A. Ward

O beau-ti-ful for spa-cious skies, for am-ber waves of grain, for

pur-ple moun-tain maj-es-ties A-bove the fruit-ed plain. A-mer-i-ca! A-

mer-i-ca! God shed His grace on thee,

broth-er-hood From sea to shin-

Continuing the subject of patriotic music, the songs "I'm a Yankee Doodle Dandy" and "You're a Grand Old Flag" were written by **Rhode Island** native, George M. Cohan.

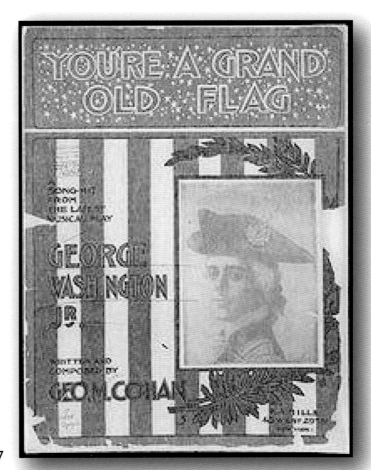

Next-door neighbor, **CONNECTICUT** is home to the Ivy League's Yale University and the US Coast Guard Academy. In 1898, Connecticut issued the first car insurance in Hartford. Connecticut was also the first state to issue permanent license plates for cars (1937).

YALE

Connecticut
879·UYP
Constitution State

Rhode Island is home to the Ivy League's Brown University, and it was Rhode Island that was first to jail a speeder, a second-time offender who was going all of 20 mph. Incidentally, the Rhode Island State Police have been voted best-dressed police officers in the country and have appeared on the *David Letterman Show*. Like brothers, Connecticut & Rhode Island work on nuclear submarines together and, years ago, *neither* state ratified the 18th Amendment, Prohibition.

BROWN

DELAWARE, home to DuPont – awarded the National Medal of Technology four times – and home to almost 50% of the Fortune 500 companies in the nation – was the very <u>first</u> state to ratify the US Constitution.

Old State House, Delaware

Delaware
It's good
being first.
THE FIRST STATE

FORTUNE
500

Rhode Island was the <u>last</u> to do so and is the 13th state. However, Rhode Island was the first state to renounce allegiance to the King of England and to offer the first armed act of rebellion (1772) against the British, burning their ship *HMS Gaspee*.

Painting (1892) of the Burning of the *HMS Gaspee* by Charles DeWolfe Brownell

Orlando, **FLORIDA** attracts more visitors than any other amusement park destination in the nation.

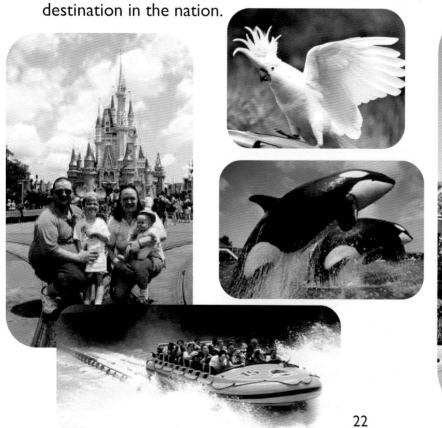

Rhode Island <u>had</u> four major amusement parks created <u>before 1900</u>. Its Rocky Point Park drew people from around the country and the world. Trolleys left every half hour to go from Providence to Warwick. At Rocky Point, President Rutherford B. Hayes became the *first president to talk on the telephone.* He spoke to Alexander Graham Bell who was 13 miles away in Providence.

23

GEORGIA, the peach state, is the chicken capital of the world and home to the Master's Golf Tournament at the Augusta National.

MASTER'S GOLF TOURNAMENT

GA 40
A31-992
PEACH STATE

GEORGIA
POULTRY PARK

Rhode Island possesses the world's first & only monument dedicated to a chicken breed, the Rhode Island Red, the state bird. In 1895, Newport, Rhode staged the first open golf tournament in the nation, which was the origin of the US Open.

25

HAWAII the widest state of the 50, is the only state to be made up <u>entirely</u> of islands – 8 major and 129 small islands.

PACIFIC OCEAN

Kure
Midway
Pearl and
Hermes Reef
NORTHWESTERN (LEEWARD) ISLANDS
Lisianski   Laysan   Gardner
French Frigate Shoals   Necker
SOUTHEASTERN (WINDWARD) ISLANDS
N
Nihoa   Kaua'i
Ni'ihau   Moloka'i
O'ahu   Maui

0   500 KILOMETERS
0   300 MILES

Hawai'i

Rhode Island, the narrowest state at only 37 miles wide, is composed of 35 islands, 12 inhabited and 23 small islands – this in addition to its mainland. Block Island (below) is probably the best known of the islands.

IDAHO is the birthplace of television (14-yar-old Philo T. Farnsworth raised in Rigby, Idaho invented it) and also home to an annual Spud Day, a festival which includes a tug of war over a deep pit of mashed potatoes.

Philo T. Farnsworth and his invention, the television. Born in Utah in 1906, raised in Idaho (where he invented TV in 1920), educated at Brigham Young University in Utah.

Rhode Island is the birthplace of Mr. Potato Head (created by Hasbro in Pawtucket) which was the first toy ever advertised on television.

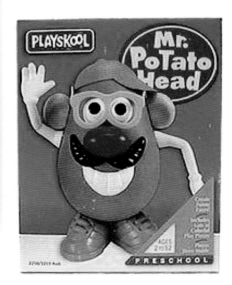

29

ILLINOIS is home of the world's first skyscraper (the Home Insurance Building, 1884) and birthplace of the silo. Chicago, Illinois has the only post office in the world under a car could be driven. This was created for the Congress Parkway to pass through.

Speaking of post offices, Providence, **Rhode Island** is home to the world's first automated post office.

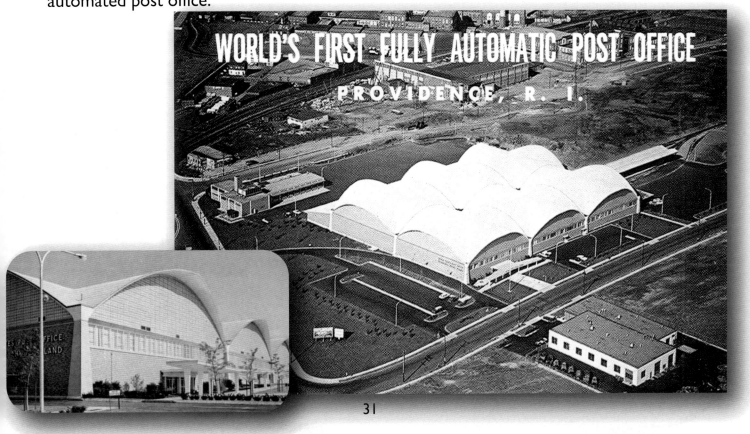

WORLD'S FIRST FULLY AUTOMATIC POST OFFICE
PROVIDENCE, R. I.

31

INDIANA is home to the first long-distance auto race in the nation in 1911 at the Indianapolis Motor Speedway and home to the Indianapolis 500, one of the greatest spectacles in sports. Parke County, Indiana is the covered bridge capital of the world with 31 covered bridges.

Cranston, **Rhode Island** was the site of the nation's first automobile race on an oval track in 1896 and later the first on an oval asphalt track. This is considered to be the first true super speedway in America – and it was sponsored by AAA.

33

IOWA, home to Quaker Oats and the Winnebago, is also home to Cornell College, the first college in the nation to promote a female to professor rank with a salary equal to that of her male colleagues. In addition, Cornell College is the first college in the nation to have its entire campus listed on the National Register of Historic Places.

34

Rhode Island, remarkably, has over 16,000 sites listed on the National Register of Historic Places, many of them also National Historic Landmarks, an enormous number for the smallest of the 50 states.

The Breakers, Newport

The Westerly Armory

Wright's Dairy Farm
North Smithfield

The Old State House
Providence

35

In 1990, **KANSAS** wheat farmers produced enough wheat to make **33 billion** loaves of bread, or enough to provide each person on earth with 6 loaves. Kansas is home to the *American Institute of Baking* and claims to have <u>among</u> its towns 27 Walnut Creeks.

Rhode Island has a total of 39 cities & towns <u>but over</u> 350 villages with some fascinating names such as Weekapaug, Apponaug, Quonochontaug, Conanicut, Conimicut, Misquamicut, Wickaboxet, Ponagansett, and Sockanosset. When a snow flake falls in Rhode Island, our citizens buy most of those Kansas bread loaves along with multiple gallons of milk.

Weekapaug
Apponaug
Quonochontaug
Conanicut
Conimicut
Misquamicut
Wickaboxet
Ponagansett
Sockanosset

Patience, Prudence, Despair, Hope,
Harmony, Jerusalem, Wyoming,
Carolina, Galilee, Moscow

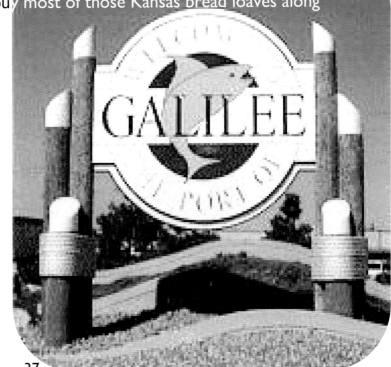

KENTUCKY is home to the internationally famous Kentucky Derby and the National Corvette Museum in Bowling Green, the city where, proudly, America's sports car, the Corvette is manufactured.

Rhode Island was the location of the first polo games played in America and the site of the first automobile parade in the nation, complete with autos decorated with flowers and birds. Polo is played today at Glen Farm in Portsmouth.

LOUISIANA, home of the Big Easy – New Orleans, is famous for its Cajun cooking and Cajun music. Louisiana has a law which says that biting someone with natural teeth is simple assault, but biting someone with false teeth is aggravated assault.

Rhode Island is famous for its Italian cooking and is well known for former Providence Mayor, Buddy Cianci, the Prince of Providence. Foster, Rhode Island has a law that says if the dentist pulls the wrong tooth from a patient's mouth, the dentist has to have that same tooth removed from his head – by the village blacksmith.

41

MAINE, the Pine Tree State and home to the most eastern <u>town</u> in the nation (Lubec), produces 90 percent of the nation's lobsters, toothpicks, and blueberries.

Rhode Island is proud of its clam cakes, grinders, New York System wieners (created in Rhode Island), Newport Creamery's Awful Awfuls, Del's Lemonade, Caserta's Wimpy Skippys, coffee cabinets, and Rhode Island clam chowder which is clear.

BEST PRODUCT
MADE IN
RHODE ISLAND:
Del's Lemonade

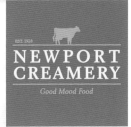

43

Annapolis, **MARYLAND** is the birthplace of Francis Scott Key (author of "The Star-Spangled Banner") and home to the US Naval Academy.

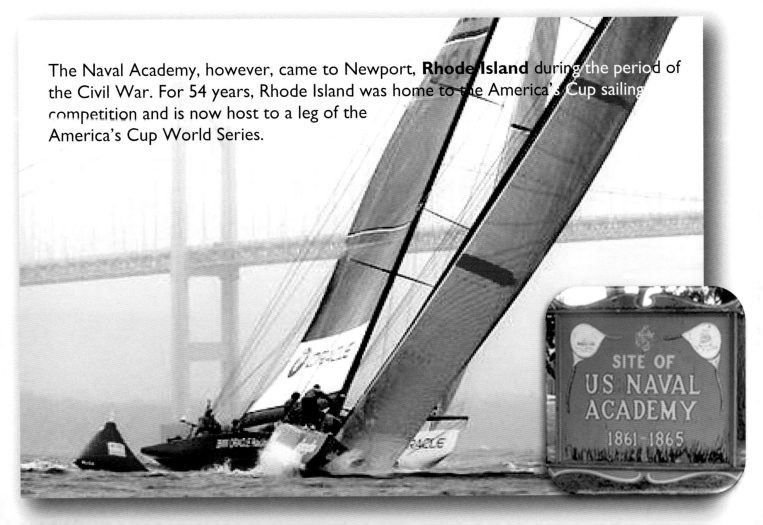

The Naval Academy, however, came to Newport, **Rhode Island** during the period of the Civil War. For 54 years, Rhode Island was home to the America's Cup sailing competition and is now host to a leg of the America's Cup World Series.

SITE OF
U.S. NAVAL
ACADEMY
1861–1865

MASSACHUSETTS, birthplace of basketball and home to the Naismith Memorial Basketball Hall of Fame, is home to the very first college in America, Harvard College, 1636.

46

The Gates at Harvard College

Rhode Island has the oldest continuing institution of its kind in the world, the US Naval War College in Newport, founded in 1884, often called the "Harvard" of war colleges. The fast break in basketball, which became famous for opening up the game, was developed by Coach Frank Keaney at the University of Rhode Island and made headlines and a movie in the 1940s.

Coach Frank Keaney
URI

MICHIGAN, the first place in the world to have a state-owned and state-operated police radio system, is home to the first land-grant university in the nation (1817) and the first institution in America to teach scientific agriculture.

Library and Museum, Michigan Agricultural College, Lansing, Mich.

FIRST OF THE LAND-GRANT COLLEGES
1855   1955
MICHIGAN STATE COLLEGE   PENNSYLVANIA STATE UNIVERSITY
3¢ UNITED STATES POSTAGE 3¢

Vintage Police Radio System

48

The University of Rhode Island is a land-grant college and one of the first four sea-grant universities with the world's only program merging disciplines of oceanography, ocean engineering, archaeology, and maritime history to study sunken ships of antiquity. Dr. Robert Ballard of the School of Oceanography, discoverer of the *Titanic*, is making **URI** global headquarters for exploring the world's oceans.

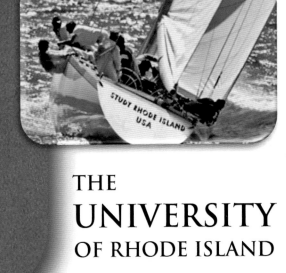

THE

UNIVERSITY
OF RHODE ISLAND

MINNESOTA, home to the SPAM® brand and the first Better Business Bureau, boasts the largest indoor shopping mall in the nation, The Mall of America® which is the size of 78 football fields and has the largest indoor theme park in the nation.

Rhode Island, on the other hand, boasts the oldest enclosed shopping mall in America, the Arcade in Providence, which opened in 1828.

MISSISSIPPI, site of the first human lung transplant and the first heart transplant surgery, was the first state in the nation to have a planned system of junior colleges. The first, Pearl River Community College, opened in 1921.

15 Community Colleges: Pearl River, Hinds. Mississippi Gulf Coast, Holmes, Mississippi Delta, Northwest, East Mississippi, Jones County, Copiah-Lincoln, East Central, Southwest, Meridian, Itawamba. Northeast, Coahoma

The Community College of **Rhode Island** is the largest two-year college in the Northeast and is rated (among two-year colleges) as one of the top five in the nation in the teaching and use of digital technology.

4 Main Campuses: Warwick, Lincoln, Providence, Newport

MISSOURI gave us the invention of iced tea at the World's Fair in St. Louis in 1904 and is home to the largest brewery in the nation (Anheuser-Busch) and the first ready-mix food to be introduced commercially in 1889 – Aunt Jemima Pancake Mix.

54

Rhode Island gave us Narragansett Beer (*Hi Neighbor*) and Kenyon's White Corn Meal which is used to make Rhode Island johnnycakes. Rhode Island is home to the only johnnycake festivals in the world.

55

The **MONTANA** Dinosaur Trail is a series of 15 dinosaur-themed museums, state parks, and other attractions that run through the entire state. A dinosaur, found in Montana, a TRex, was found to contain transparent, flexible, and hollow blood vessels with round microscopic structures inside. The structures look like cells, leading scientists to believe that some dinosaur soft tissues may keep a portion of their flexibility, elasticity, and resilience even after 68 million years.

THE MONTANA
DINOSAUR TRAIL

Sixty-eight million years later, came the Rhode Island Red. The collagen preserved in TRex bones has been broken down and analyzed with a mass spectrometer – and found to be a very close match to chickens. TRex was *only* an overgrown chicken, while the Red is the *Rhode Island State Bird*.

I'm from RI. Where are you from?

NEBRASKA developed and first used the 911 system. The remarkable Chimney Rock in Nebraska is the most famous landmark on the Oregon-California Trail. Nebraska is home to the National Arbor Day Foundation and the birthplace of Arbor Day (founded in 1872 and celebrated the last Friday in April).

Arbor Day Foundation®

The Morton Oak at Arbor Day Farr

On the nautical side, **Rhode Island** is birthplace of the US Navy and the US Navy Seabees. Rhode Island's Esek Hopkins was the first commander in chief of the Continental Navy.

The Seabee emblem was created by Frank Iafrate of North Providence.

The Seabee in Davisville at the Seabee Museum.
Seabee (CB) = Construction Battalion (note the tools & weapon)

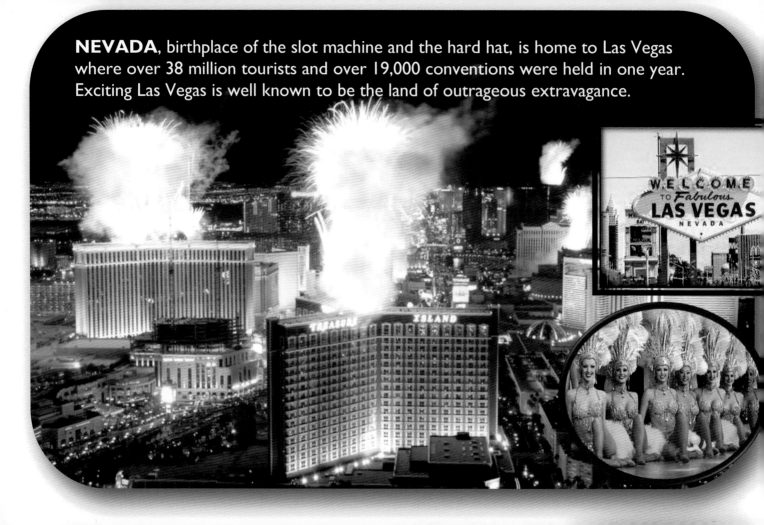

NEVADA, birthplace of the slot machine and the hard hat, is home to Las Vegas where over 38 million tourists and over 19,000 conventions were held in one year. Exciting Las Vegas is well known to be the land of outrageous extravagance.

Rhode Island is home to the outrageously extravagant Newport mansions representing conspicuous consumption. These mansions were called "summer cottages" and used for only a few weeks in the summer.

NEW HAMPSHIRE, site of the first potato planted in America, has its granite State House in Concord, the oldest state house in which the legislature still sits in its original chambers (1819).

THE NATION'S OLDEST STATE HOUSE IN WHICH THE LEGISLATURE STILL OCCUPIES ITS ORIGINAL CHAMBERS

1819   JUNE 2   1969

62

LIVE FREE OR DIE
104 1608
10   *New* HAMPSHIRE

Foster, **Rhode Island** claims the oldest town house (town hall) in continuous use in the nation, built in 1796.

NEW JERSEY, diner capital of the nation and most densely populated state, boasts the most diners in the whole world.

Rhode Island boasts the *creation* of the diner by Walter Scott who began with a lunch wagon pulled by a horse. The Modern Diner in Pawtucket, RI (1858) was the first diner in America to be listed on the National Register and was driven in 2008 to New York to *The Today Show* on which it appeared with Meredith Vieira, a Rhode Island native. Rhode Island is the second most densely populated state.

NEW MEXICO is home to the world's largest international balloon festival (Albuquerque). In New Mexico, only three-quarters of the roads are paved because the state is so dry that the roads don't wash away.

Welcome
— to —
NEW MEXICO
Land of Enchantment

Rhode Island tries hard to pave its roads. In this year's highway ratings, New Mexico ranked 4th in the nation, while Rhode Island ranked 40th.

NEW YORK is home to the Rochester Red Wings, the United States Military Academy (West Point), and some of the nation's tallest buildings. However, it is also home to the world's smallest church in Oneida at 3.5'x6'. The non-denominational chapel is on an island and has room to accommodate only the minister, bride, & groom. The rest of the wedding party watches from boats or on shore.

UNITED STATES

MILITARY ACADEM

Rhode Island is home to the first Baptist church in America (1636), the oldest synagogue in America (Touro, 1763), and the first Quaker Meeting House in the nation (1699). A note about New York & RI: it was the Rochester Red Wings of New York vs. the Pawtucket Red Sox of Rhode Island who played in the longest game in baseball history – 33 innings (Wade Boggs & Cal Ripken, Jr. played against each other). The PawSox won.

NORTH CAROLINA is the furniture capital of the world with makers such as Broyhill, Thomasville, and La-Z-Boy. Additionally, Winston-Salem, North Carolina is the birthplace of those remarkable and sinful Krispy Kreme doughnuts.

Rhode Island holds the world's record for the number of doughnut stores per capita. It is Rhode Island furniture, however, that is renowned throughout the world. A secretary, made by John Goddard of Newport, still holds the record for an American piece of furniture sold at auction – $12.1 million in 1989.

NORTH DAKOTA grows the most sunflowers of any state in the nation, while the state flower is not the sunflower but the wild prairie rose. North Dakota is home to the largest French fry fest in the nation. Two North Dakota laws of interest say it is illegal to lie down and fall asleep with your shoes on and if you wear a hat while dancing, you can be jailed.

Rhode Island grows giant pumpkins – over 1700 pounds and has won the world championship numerous times. North Dakotans should beware: Rhode Islanders are known to put vinegar on their French fries.

OHIO, rubber capital of the world (Akron), installed the first traffic light in America in Cleveland and is home to the Pro Football Hall of Fame (Canton).

Rhode Island boasts the first NFL team, the (World Champion) Providence Steam Roller, to play its home games in a bicycle-racing stadium – and first to host an NFL game at night under floodlights. Cleveland, Ohio was the first city in the world to be lighted electrically, while Pelham Street in Newport was the first street in the nation to have gas-illuminated street lights.

FIRST STREET IN THE
UNITED STATES
TO BE LIGHTED WITH GAS
INSTALLED BY
DAVID MELVILLE 1805

PROVIDENCE
1922
STEAM ROLLERS

OKLAHOMA, the last state to legalize tattooing, was the first state in the nation to install parking meters (1935) and the state in which the "Yield" sign was invented and first used (Tulsa). Oklahoma is home to Fort Sill, the largest field artillery complex in the free world.

Rhode Island, on the other hand, is home to the nation's largest coastal fortification, Fort Adams in Newport. A note on Rhode Island driving: RhodeIslanders are known to be feisty with yield signs and almost never use directional signals ("blinkers").

OREGON, one of the top 10 bicycling communities in the nation (Eugene), has the world's largest & most comprehensive collection of carousel horses at the International Museum of Carousel Art on the Hood River. The collection includes over 110 carved animals.

Rhode Island has the oldest continuously operating carousel in the nation (Watch Hill Flying Horse Carousel in Westerly). In 1880, Newport, Rhode Island hosted the first national meet of bicyclists, the League of American Wheelmen (*Bicyclists*).

PENNSYLVANIA, home to the US Army War College, is the chocolate capital of the nation as well as home to Punxutawney Phil, the ground hog that determines a longer winter or early spring.

Rhode Island boasts Nibbles Woodaway, the big blue bug on top of the roof of New England Pest Control (off Route 95), which is **928** times actual termite size. Nibbles has appeared in a number of Hollywood movies.

SOUTH CAROLINA, 8th of the 13 colonies and home to the Marine Corps Recruit Depot on Parris Island, is home to one of the first 18-hole golf courses in the nation as well as one of the oldest ballparks in the nation, Duncan Park Stadium (1926), where Joe DiMaggio and Lou Gehrig once played an exhibition game.

82

Rhode Island is home to the first 9-hole golf course in the nation and, like South Carolina, home to one of the oldest ballparks, Cardines Field with a stadium built in 1877. Rhode Island can boast the first professional baseball world champions, the Providence Grays – and Babe Ruth briefly played with them.

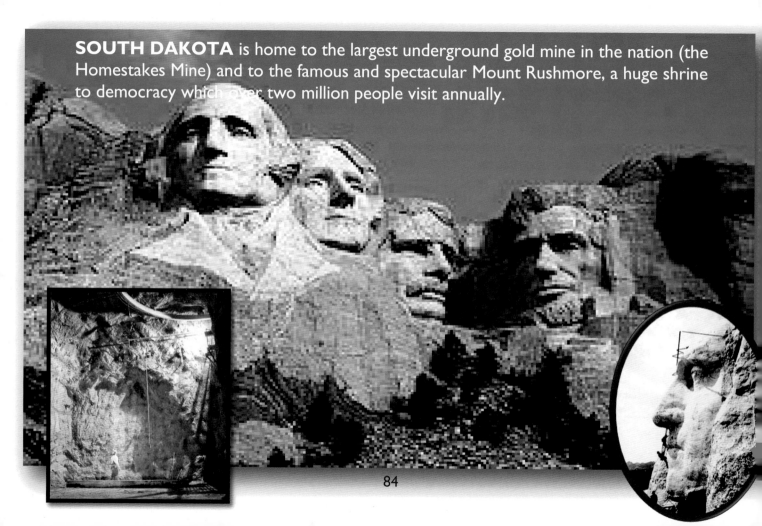

SOUTH DAKOTA is home to the largest underground gold mine in the nation (the Homestakes Mine) and to the famous and spectacular Mount Rushmore, a huge shrine to democracy which over two million people visit annually.

84

Rhode Island is home to the oldest known monument to veterans in the United States (Nine Men's Misery Monument in Cumberland) erected in memory of the colonists killed in King Phillip's War in 1676. Cumberlandite is the state rock.

TENNESSEE, birthplace of country music (Bristol), is home to Gibson guitars and the oldest, continuously operated African-America bank in the United States, Citizens Savings Bank & Trust Company founded in 1904.

Rhode Island is home to the oldest community bank in the nation, The Washington Trust Company. This bank was founded in 1800 and produced the very first bank notes with a picture of George Washington on them.

ROUNDUP ON KING RANCH

20 CENTS
JULY 8, 1957

The King Ranch in **TEXAS**, at 1300 square miles, is larger than the State of Rhode Island. Texas, which has flown under six different flags, once had 5 temporary state capitals at one time.

The Six Flags of Texas

88

Rhode Island once had 5 permanent capitals at one time with a rotating legislature (until 1854): Providence, Newport, East Greenwich, Bristol, and South Kingstown.

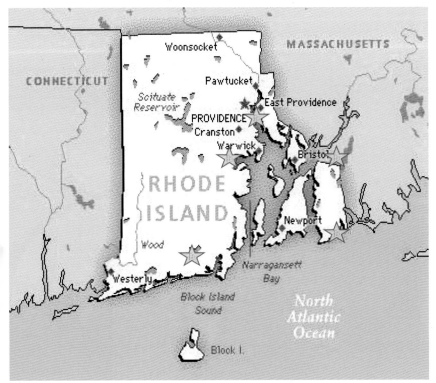

UTAH is home to the highest peaks in the lower 48 states. These gorgeous mountains helped the state become home to the XIX (19th) Winter **Olympic Games.** Utah is one of only two states in which a majority of its **population belongs to a single religious body (Mormon).**

Rhode Island is the other (Roman Catholic). For several years, Rhode Island hosted the Gravity Games in Providence. Rhode Island's highest point is Jerimoth Hill in Foster at a whopping 812' above sea level.

91

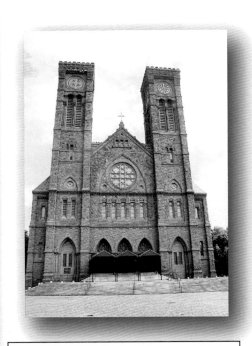

Cathedral of Saints Peter & Paul
Providence

VERMONT, largest producer of maple syrup in the nation, was the only state, until 1996, without a WalMart. Vermont is home to Ben & Jerry's and Vermonters love their special ice cream.

Rhode Island is home to Autocrat and Eclipse coffee syrup. Rhode Islanders love their coffee milk, the official state drink.

VIRGINIA is home to President Washington's Mount Vernon and President Jefferson's Monticello. It is also home to the United States Atlantic Fleet and the largest office building in the world, the Pentagon in Arlington.

Rhode Island is birthplace of the modest Quonset Hut, developed at Davisville in North Kingstown. The hut was a light-weight, prefabricated structure of corrugated galvanized steel which could be easily shipped anywhere. Over 150,000 Quonset huts were manufactured during World War II.

WASHINGTON is the birthplace of Father's Day (1910) as well as home to leading corporations such as Microsoft , Starbucks, and Amazon.com.

Starbucks
Coffee

amazon.com

MICROSOFT

Rhode Island is headquarters for the largest pharmacy health-care provider in the nation, *CVS Caremark*; the oldest mutual insurer of automobiles in the nation, *Amica*; the oldest writing instrument designer & manufacturer in the Western Hemisphere, *A.T. Cross Company*; the second largest toy maker in the US, *Hasbro* – maker of GI Joe, (the world's first action figure), Transformers, Scrabble, Twister, the Easy-Bake Oven, Mr. Potato Head, and Monopoly (the world's best-selling game).

And two of RI's smaller but all-time favorites:

WEST VIRGINIA, birthplace of Mother's Day (first observed in 1908), is home to the only building in the world made entirely of coal. It is also the birthplace of outdoor advertising (Wheeling, c. 1908) and was the first state in the nation to have a sales tax.

Rhode Island captures the essence of taxing and advertising with its Individual Income Tax Return form (RI-1040) which is the only state tax return with frowning and smiley faces.

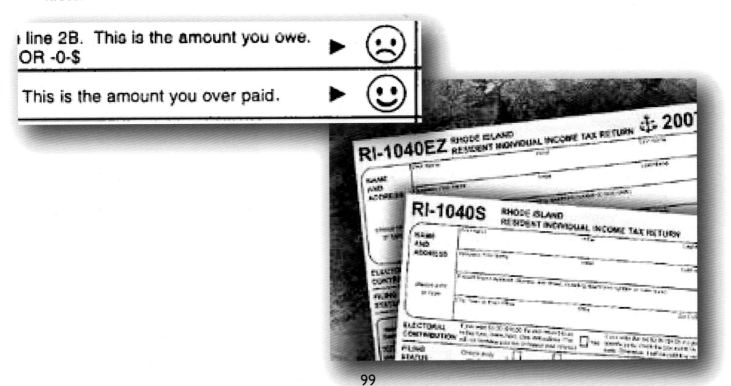

line 2B. This is the amount you owe. ☹

OR -0-$

This is the amount you over paid. ☺

RI-1040EZ RHODE ISLAND RESIDENT INDIVIDUAL INCOME TAX RETURN 200

RI-1040S RHODE ISLAND RESIDENT INDIVIDUAL INCOME TAX RETURN

WISCONSIN, loon capital of the world and dairy capital of the nation, is home to the world's largest music festival, Milwaukee's Summerfest.

MILWAUKEE

Summerfest

The World's Largest Music Festival

Rhode Island is home to the Newport Jazz Festival (first jazz festival in the nation, 1954), the Newport Folk Festival, and the Newport Music Festival (classical) which is acclaimed as one of the Top 100 events in North America.

101

WYOMING, home to Yellowstone National Park and the first national monument (Devil's Tower, 1906), is the first state to give women the right to vote and stick to it. Wyoming has several old laws still on the books. First, you cannot take a picture of a rabbit from January to April without a permit. Second, to honor women, anyone in Wyoming can be arrested for spitting in front of a woman.

Proudly, **Rhode Island** was the first state to have a woman State Attorney General (Arlene Violet) and the first state to have a woman newspaper editor, Ann Smith Franklin of *The Newport Mercury*. Rhode Island was the first place in the world to appoint a woman fire chief, Nancy Crawford Allen of Warwick. On the note of unusual laws, Rhode Island <u>almost</u> had a tax law implemented in 1976 when one of the state representatives proposed a $2.00 tax on sex to replace to the state income tax.

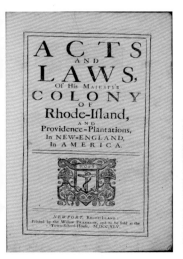

There are fifty amazing states, and Rhode Island is certainly one of them. The United States is nothing less than remarkable because of the people – their work ethic, their imagination, their individuality, and their courage.

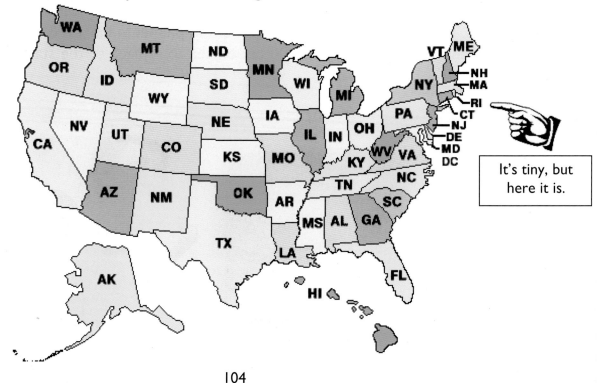

It's tiny, but here it is.

When you have finished reading this book, it is hoped that you will fondly recall Rhode Island and experience its many exceptional sites and treasures. To help you remember: when you pull out a one-dollar bill, you will see the famous portrait of George Washington. It was the artist, Gilbert Stuart who painted that iconic picture. Gilbert Stuart was born in North Kingstown, Rhode Island.

The Gilbert Stuart Birthplace

Rhode Island is the 13th and smallest state – the state with the longest name – *Rhode Island and Providence Plantations*, and the shortest motto, *Hope*. May a little knowledge about Rhode Island and its 49 brother states give us all a significant amount of pride in the United States of America.

Recognition & Appreciation for Permissions

Artistic images (as below) of the Sherman Windmill of Prescott Farm & other RI historic places created by John G. Humble and from the book, *Rhode Island's Friendly Faces* by Roberta Mudge Humble © 2007.